SILLY RIDDLES

Chosen and illustrated
by Mik Brown

WARWICK PRESS
New York/London/Toronto/Sydney
1988

For Toby, Jacob, Lucie, Theo and Zoe

Published in 1988 by Warwick Press,
387 Park Avenue South, New York, New York 10016.
First published in 1987 by Kingfisher Books Ltd.
Copyright © Mik Brown 1987.

Library of Congress Catalog Card No. 88-50129
ISBN 0-531-19048-X

Printed in Spain

What do you call a gorilla wearing earphones?

Anything—he can't hear you.

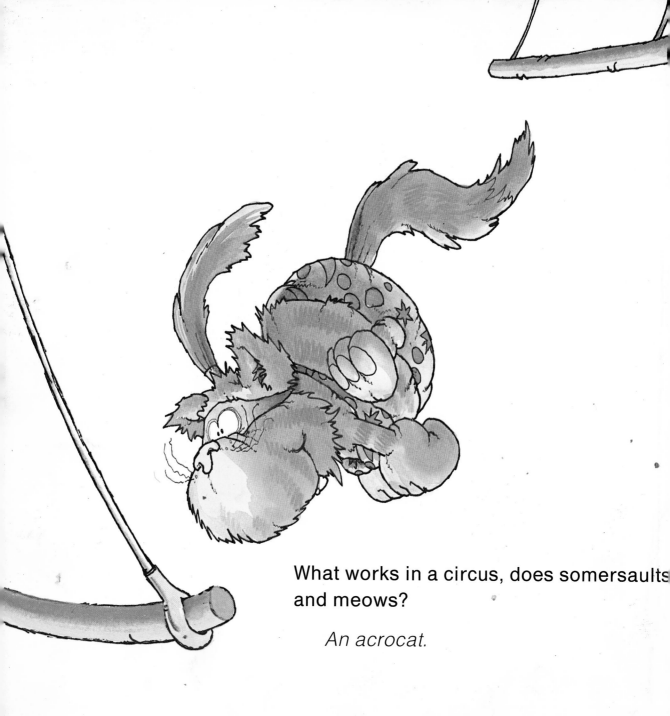

What works in a circus, does somersaults and meows?

An acrocat.

Why does a dog wag
its tail?

*Because no one will
wag it for him.*

TIC!
TOC!

What goes tick tock, bow wow,
tick tock, bow wow?

A watch dog.

What's black and white and has sixteen wheels?

A zebra on roller skates.

Where do you find hippos?

It depends where you left them.

Why did the mother kangaroo scold her baby?

For eating biscuits in bed.

What do you call someone with a seagull on his head?

Cliff.

Why is it hard for leopards to hide?

Because they're always spotted.

What do you get if you cross
a snake with a magician?

Abra da cobra.

What do you get if you cross
a chicken with a cement
mixer?

A brick-layer

What do you get if you cross
a snowman with a tiger?

Frostbite.

GRRRR!

What do you get if you cross
a parrot with an alligator?

*Something that bites your hand
off and says, "Who's a pretty
boy then?"*

WHO'S
A
PRETTY
BOY
THEN?

What do you get if you cross
a bear with a skunk?

Winnie the Pooh.

What do you get if you cross
an elephant with a kangaroo?

*Great big holes
all over Australia.*

THUD!

GULP!

"Mummy mummy, I've just swallowed my mouth organ!"

"Just be glad you don't play the piano."

What kind of noise annoys an oyster?

A noisy noise annoys an oyster.

QUIET!

GIRL: "I've found a penguin."
BOY: "Why don't you take it to the zoo?"
GIRL: "I took it to the zoo yesterday. Today we're going to the movies."

What pet makes the loudest noise?

A trumpet.

What goes OOM OOM?

A cow walking backward.

FIRST COW: "Moo."
SECOND COW: "Baa-a-a."
FIRST COW: "What do you mean Baa-a-a?"
SECOND COW: "I'm learning a foreign language."

What do you get from a
bad-tempered shark?

As far away as possible.

YIKES!

How do you stop a skunk smelling?

Hold its nose.

What do skunks have that no other animals have?

Baby skunks.

What is black and white
and very noisy?

A skunk with a drum kit.

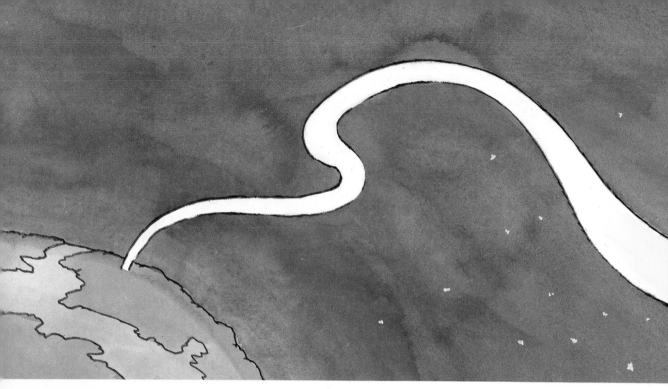

How do you get a baby astronaut to sleep?

You rock-et.

What did the astronaut
see in his frying pan?

*An unidentified
frying object.*

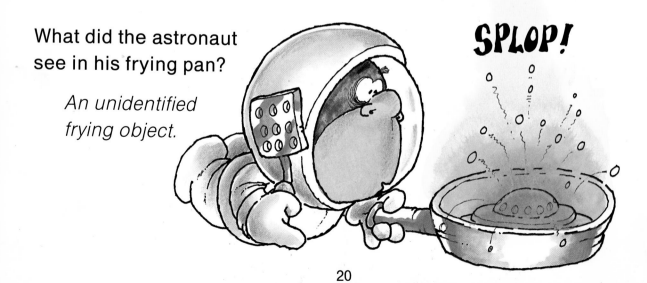

What do astronauts eat for lunch?

Launch meat sandwiches.

Why did the monster
knit herself three
socks?

*Because
she grew
another foot.*

What is the best way to speak to a monster?

From a long distance.

Why are monsters forgetful?

*Because everything you tell
them goes in one ear
and out the others.*

Where do you take a frog
with bad eyesight?

To the hoptician.

What's green and can jump
a mile a minute?

A frog with hiccups.

What's scaly,
has a hard shell
and bounces?

*A turtle on
a pogo stick.*

What was the turtle doing
on the freeway?

About 150 inches an hour.

Where did Napoleon keep his armies?

Up his sleevies.

What's green and hairy and goes up and down?

A gooseberry in a lift.

Where did Humpty Dumpty leave his hat?

Humpty dumped his hat on the wall.

What is the biggest ant?

An elephant.

Why did the elephant paint himself different colors?

Because he wanted to hide in the crayon box.

What time is it when an elephant sits on a chair?

Time to get another chair.

What's green and dangerous and good at sums?

A crocodile with a calculator.

What's the differenc[e] between a crocodile and a mailbox?

If you don't know watch out when you mail a letter!

30

What bee can never be understood?

A mumble bee.

How can you tell
which end
of a worm
is which?

*Tickle its middle
and see which end
smiles.*

What has two arms, two wings, two tails, three heads, three bodies, and eight legs?

A man on a horse holding a chicken.